Fiction Teacher's Book 5
Wendy Body

Series Editor: Wendy Body

Pearson Education Limited
Edinburgh Gate
Harlow
Essex
CM20 2JE
England and Associated Companies throughout the World

ISBN 0582 48843 5
First published 2001
Second impression 2002

Printed in Great Britain by Scotprint, Haddington
Designed by AMR, Bramley, Hants

The Publisher's policy is to use paper manufactured from sustainable forests.

Edinburgh Gate
Harlow, Essex

If you wish to enlarge any of the Shared Writing Examples for use in your teaching, you may do so.

Contents

Year 5 Fiction Summary Chart

Unit in Resource Book	Text objective	Sentence level objective links	Unit of work
Term 1 Unit 1 *Viola Angotti*	**T14** to map out texts showing development and structure	**S7** to understand how dialogue is set out	Map texts to show structure
Term 1 Unit 2 *Viola Angotti*	**T15** to write new scenes or characters into a story, in the manner of the writer	**S3** to discuss, proof-read and edit their own writing for clarity and correctness ...	Write in the manner of the author
Term 1 Unit 3 Writing a Reading Journal	**T13** to record their ideas predictions about a book, e.g. through a reading log or journal	**S5** to understand the difference between direct and reported speech ...	Write in a reading journal
Term 1 Unit 4 *Evacuee*	**T16** to convey feelings, reflections or moods in a poem through the careful choice of words and phrases	**S3** to discuss, proof-read and edit their own writing for clarity and correctness ...	Write a poem conveying feelings
Term 1 Unit 5 Writing Metaphors	**T17** to write metaphors from original ideas or from similes		Write metaphors
Term 1 Unit 6 *Inside the Labyrinth*	**T19** to annotate a section of playscript as a preparation for performance		Annotate a playscript
Term 1 Unit 7 *Inside the Labyrinth*	**T18** to write own playscript, applying conventions learned from reading; include production notes	**S6** to understand the need for punctuation as an aid to the reader	Write a playscript
Term 1 Unit 8 *Inside the Labyrinth*	**T20** to evaluate the script and performance for their dramatic interest and impact		Evaluate the playscript
Term 2 Unit 9 *Tee-rah-wah's Gift*	**T1** to identify and classify the features of myths	**S5** to use punctuation effectively to signpost meaning in longer and more complex sentences	Identify myths

Term 2 Unit 10 *Tee-rah-wah's Gift*	**T11** to write own versions of legends, myths and fables using structures and themes identified in reading		Write a myth
Term 2 Unit 11 *Tee-rah-wah's Gift*	**T13** to review and edit writing to produce a final form, matched to the needs of an identified reader	**S3** to understand how writing can be adapted for different audiences and purposes	Adapt writing for a different audience
Term 2 Unit 12 *Overheard on a Saltmarsh*	**T12** to use the structures of poems read to write extensions based on these, e.g. additional verses or substituting own words and ideas		Write an extension to the poem
Term 2 Unit 13 What Do All Stories Have? Revising Writing	**T13** to review and edit writing to produce a final form, matched to the needs of an identified reader	**S5** to use punctuation effectively to signpost meaning in longer and more complex sentences	Revise own writing
Term 2 Unit 14 *Counting the Stars*	**T14** to make notes of story outline as preparation for oral storytelling	**S6** to be aware of the differences between spoken and written language ...	Make notes for oral storytelling
Term 3 Unit 15 *Something wrong with the stove?*	**T8** to record predictions, questions, reflections while reading		Record predictions and reflections
Term 3 Unit 16 *Something wrong with the stove?*	**T9** to write in the style of the author, e.g. writing on to complete a section, resolve a conflict ...	**S7** to use connectives to link clauses within sentences and to link sentences in longer texts	Write in the style of the author
Term 3 Unit 17 *Something wrong with the stove?*	**T7** to write from another character's point of view, e.g. retelling an incident in letter form		Write from another character's point of view
Term 3 Unit 18 Writing About A Story	**T10** to write discursively about a novel or story, e.g. to describe, explain or comment on it	**S4** to use punctuation marks accurately in complex sentences	Write about a story
Term 3 Unit 19 *The Sound Collector*	**T11** to use performance poems as models to write ... poetry		Write a polished poem from a model
Term 3 Unit 20 Standard English: *My Bruvver*	**T11** to produce poetry in polished forms through revising, redrafting and presentation	**S1** to secure the basic conventions of standard English	Rewrite a poem in standard English

Introduction

What Is *Pelican Shared Writing*?

Pelican Shared Writing is an easy-to-use resource for teaching shared writing. It comprises ten packs: one Fiction and one Non-Fiction pack for each year group for Years 2, 3, 4, 5 and 6. Each pack contains:
- one *Writing Resource Book*
- one *Teacher's Book* with copymasters
- a large sheet of acetate and a Pelican page clip

Each *Writing Resource Book* offers 20 units of work which cover all the NLS writing composition objectives for the year group. Each writing composition objective forms one unit of work. Links are also made to appropriate sentence level objectives.

Although *Pelican Shared Writing* stands alone, it has links to *Pelican Guided Reading and Writing* in terms of objectives and tasks and there are content links to *Pelican Big Books*.

The Writing Resource Books
- Each 48-page big book is split into three parts – one for each term's teaching objectives.
- Shared writing is rooted in shared reading, and so the *Writing Resource Book* contains the texts which not only provide the starting point for writing, but also act as models of the genre to be studied. Story plans and writing frames are sometimes included as well.
- Quotes about the writing process from professional children's writers feature on the inside back cover of some of the *Fiction Writing Resource Books* to initiate discussions on writing.
- Each book comes with a large sheet of acetate and a Pelican page clip for text marking and writing.

The Teacher's Books

The *Teacher's Book* in each pack contains:
- teaching pages for each unit of work with detailed, step-by-step advice on what to do in each shared writing session. There are also examples of completed activities which teachers can use to guide the class in composing a text. Units will usually take more than one shared writing session to complete.
- a small number of copymasters e.g. writing frames, character planners. These are for general use and can also be applied to other texts and writing activities
- copymaster versions of all the *Writing Resource Book* texts. These can be used to make overhead transparencies and in instances where it is helpful for children to have their own copy of a text e.g. for annotation.

The *Non-Fiction Teacher's Book* has a summary of links to other areas of the curriculum on the last page.

Teaching Shared Writing

Pelican Shared Writing complements the National Literacy Strategy's *Grammar for Writing* guidance. *Pelican Shared Writing* concentrates on delivering the text level writing composition objectives whereas *Grammar for Writing* concentrates on sentence level objectives. *Pelican Shared Writing* adopts a similar approach to shared writing which may be summarised as follows:

Key features of shared writing
- Make explicit how purpose and audience determine form and style.
- Link the writing to specific objectives.
- Rehearse sentences orally before writing.
- Discuss and explain alternatives and choices.
- Keep re-reading to maintain flow, meaning and consistency.
- Involve children in the revision and editing.

Shared Writing Techniques:

Teacher demonstration

The teacher composes and writes, modelling for children how to compose a particular text type or tackle a writing activity. He/she thinks aloud, rehearses choices before writing, explains choices and makes changes. The children do not contribute to the composition but they are invited to offer opinions on, for example, the choice of words or sentence construction. Demonstration time will vary according to the text and children's competence, but avoid spending too long – children need to try things for themselves.

Teacher scribing

The teacher acts as scribe and builds on the initial demonstration by asking the children to make contributions to the composition or task. The teacher guides, focuses, explains and challenges the contributions e.g. *Why did you choose that word? That's a really good sentence construction because ...* While children could make their contributions orally by putting up their hands, it is preferable for them to use whiteboards (in pairs or individually) which ensures participation by all children. It is also advisable to take "time out" i.e. children turn to each other in pairs and discuss possibilities for 30 seconds or so.

Supported Composition

Supported composition is preparation for independent writing. Children compose a limited amount of text using whiteboards or notebooks – in pairs or individually. Their alternatives are reviewed and discussed and choices and changes made. Some differentiation can be achieved by seating children in their ability groups and asking one group to compose one sentence orally, another to write one or two sentences and a third to write several sentences. Supported composition will enable you to identify those children who will need to repeat or continue the task in guided writing i.e. those who need greater support.

Shared writing is the most powerful means of improving and developing children's writing skills. But they will not develop into proficient writers unless, firstly, they are given sufficient TIME to practise the skills and craft of writing for themselves, and secondly, they receive the FEEDBACK which will help them evaluate what they have done and learn from it.

Teaching a *Pelican Shared Writing* unit of work

Support for each step will be found on the teaching pages

Discussing the Text for each unit

- Introduce the task and the objective
- Read the text in the Resource Book with the class and discuss the content
- Draw out features of the genre

Shared Writing

- Demonstrate or model the particular features of the writing
- Scribe and guide the pupils' contributions
- Continue with supported composition by children working in pairs
- Check the children's learning

Independent Writing

- Children complete the writing task.
- They consolidate their learning by carrying out another similar task.

Checking the Objective

- Determine children's understanding of the objective and how far they can apply their knowledge by evaluating their writing.

Revisiting the Objective

- If needs be, repeat the whole process using the suggested activity.

Note: A *Pelican Shared Writing* CD-ROM is available for use alongside each year's work. For further details, please see the section on ICT, overleaf.

ICT and Pelican Shared Writing

ICT may be used by all pupils to support writing skills. The word processor or desktop publishing package can enable the child to focus on the development of ideas and the manipulation of the written word without the physical constraints imposed by the handwriting process. The ease of editing, the spell-checking facilities and the ability to move text around the page make ICT support programs valuable tools to include within the writing repertoire. Writing tasks offer the ideal opportunity to integrate and apply those ICT skills being developed in the ICT curriculum.

Almost any writing task may be approached using ICT as an optional writing tool. These writing tasks will offer strong links with the ICT curriculum, which aims that pupils should:

- 'develop their ability to apply their IT capability and ICT to support their use of language and communication'
- 'pass on ideas by communicating, presenting and exchanging information'
- 'develop language skills eg in systematic writing and in presenting their own ideas'
- 'be creative and persistent'
- 'explore their attitudes towards ICT, its value for themselves … and their awareness of its advantages and limitations'

(QCA Scheme of Work for ICT, Aims and Purposes)

The 'Communicating' strand for ICT is inextricably linked with developing literacy. Computer access is a great resource for independent, group and class work, and is too valuable a tool to remain unused during the development of literacy skills. It is a great motivator and encourages collaborative work that can become more focused as children's attention is extended.

Within the suggested Year 5 Fiction *Pelican Shared Writing* activities, there are some clear links with units from the QCA Scheme of Work for ICT, particularly Unit 4A 'Writing for Different Audiences'. This unit focuses on text manipulation skills, and the writing activities offer ideal opportunities for their application. If graphics are used in documents, then the skills from Unit 3A 'Combining Text and Graphics', may also be applied.

Links to the most relevant National Curriculum Programmes of Study for ICT are listed in the table opposite.

The differentiated writing frames for Year 5 (Fiction and Non-Fiction) are available on the CD-ROM entitled *Pelican Shared Writing Year 5* (ISBN 0582 50988 2), which can be easily installed on any machine supporting Microsoft Word. Here they may be adapted, should you so wish, to suit your particular needs. The CD-ROM also provides cross-referencing charts for both Writing and ICT targets, including the ICT Programme of Study references and links to the QCA Scheme of Work for ICT – collated and readily available for inclusion in planning records.

Year 5 Fiction
Relevant objectives from the ICT Programme of Study

Pupils should be taught:

1a
to talk about what information they need and how they can find and use it (*for example, searching the internet or a CD-ROM, using printed material, asking people*)

2a
how to develop and refine ideas by bringing together, organising and reorganising text, tables, images and sound as appropriate (*for example, desktop publishing, multimedia presentations*)

3a
how to share and exchange information in a variety of forms, including e-mail (*for example, displays, posters, animations, musical compositions*)

3b
to be sensitive to the needs of the audience and think carefully about the content and quality when communicating information (*for example, work for presentation to other pupils, writing for parents, publishing on the internet*).

4b
to describe and talk about the effectiveness of their work with ICT, comparing it with other methods and considering the effect it has on others (*for example, the impact made by a desktop-published newsletter or poster*)

National Curriculum for England, ICT Programme of Study

Term 1 Unit of work 1:

Map texts to show structure

Writing objective

T14: To map out texts showing development and structure

Links to sentence/word level work

S7: To understand how dialogue is set out

Text Copymasters: C5–9

Discussing the Text

- Tell the children that they are going to read an extract from a novel they may already know called 'The Eighteenth Emergency' by Betsy Byars.
- Read together the text entitled 'Viola Angotti' (pages 2 to 9).
- Discuss what the extract implies about the boys' attitude to girls and what the children think of this and the boys' behaviour.
- *Which vocabulary tells you that this story is American?* (trash cans, school yard, sidewalk, garbage can, principal)
- What does the nickname 'Mouse' suggest about the storyteller?
- How do Mouse's feelings change through the extract?
- *What makes this extract humorous?*
- What can the children tell you about the way dialogue is set out from this extract?

Shared Writing

Session 1

Teacher demonstration

- Tell the children that you are going to chart the structure or development of the extract by looking at each paragraph of 'Viola Angotti' and saying what it is about and the author's purpose.
- Either use Copymaster C1 or draw out a chart as in the Shared Writing Example (opposite).
- Read the first paragraph (page 2). Fill in the first Content box as in the Shared Writing Example opposite.
- *What the author is doing here is introducing the idea of the boys deciding to put the girls into the trash cans. So I'm going to write …* (See the Shared Writing Example).
- Repeat with the next paragraph (pages 2 to 3). Ask the children if they agree with what you have written.

Teacher scribing

- Ask for suggestions as to what you should write under Content for paragraph 3 (page 4) and scribe.
- Ask the children to take time out to discuss the author's purpose in pairs, using the Shared Writing Example to guide the class if needs be. Take suggestions, select and scribe.
- Fill in the boxes for paragraphs 4 and 5 in a similar way.

Shared Writing Example: Structure Chart

Paragraph	Content	The Author's Purpose
1 (page 2)	the boys decide to put the girls in the trash cans	• introduction to the main idea
2 (pages 2–3)	Mouse chases the girls and catches Viola Angotti	• show Mouse's feelings of strength and power • introduce Viola Angotti
3 (page 4)	Mouse realises who he has caught and that he'll need help	• give first clue the Viola Angotti is no ordinary girl • show how Mouse's feelings start to change
4 (page 4)	Mouse needs help; doesn't know he's alone because other boys have been caught by the principal	• give explanation to the reader (why none of the other boys come to help)
5 (page 5)	Mouse shouts for help	• show Mouse's growing anxiety
6 (page 6)	Viola Angotti stands up to Mouse	• provide more detail about Viola Angotti's character
7 (page 8)	Mouse shouts for help again	• show Mouse's desperation
8 (page 8)	Viola Angotti hits Mouse. Mouse is sick	• turn things round so that the victim becomes the aggressor
9 (page 9)	Viola Angotti walks off and leaves Mouse in a crumpled heap	• emphasise Viola Angotti's strength and power • add humour

Supported composition

- Ask the children (in pairs or individually) to write what should go under Content for paragraph 6 (page 6). Take suggestions, select and scribe.
- Ask the children to discuss and then write the author's purpose. Take suggestions, select and scribe. Again, use the Shared Writing Example to guide the class if necessary.
- Repeat for paragraph 7 (page 8).
- Read what has been written so far. Keep for Unit of work 2.

Independent Writing

- Using Copymaster C1, children should finish charting the extract. They should start at the top because the rest of the space will be needed in Unit of Work 2.
- Use Copymaster C1 to chart another story/extract.

Checking Children's Learning

- Have children been able to distinguish between the content and what the author was doing in each paragraph?
- Were they able to complete the final paragraphs along the lines of the Shared Writing Example?

Revisiting the Objective

- Create a similar chart, with three columns headed 'Paragraph', 'Mouse's Feelings' and 'Viola's Feelings', which shows the development and changes in the two characters' feelings.

Term 1 Unit of work 2:

Write in the manner of the author

Writing objective

T15: To write new scenes or characters into a story, in the manner of the writer, maintaining consistency of character and style, using paragraphs to organise and develop detail

Links to sentence/word level work

S3: To discuss, proof-read and edit their own writing for clarity and correctness …

Text Copymasters: C5–9

Discussing the text

- Re-read the extract.
- Discuss features of Betsy Byars' writing. For example: *use of American words*, e.g. school yard, sidewalk, principal; *use of exaggeration for effect and humour*, e.g. 'Viola Angotti could be heavyweight champion of the world' (page 4); *use of natural and realistic direct speech* (try reading it aloud in an American accent); *variety of sentence length, but short sentences often used for impact*, e.g. top of page 4; *small descriptive details*, e.g. 'crumpled body' (page 9); *little use of figurative language, similes or metaphors*.

Shared Writing

NB This may take more than one session

Teacher scribing

- Tell the children that they are going to try and copy Betsy Byars' style and extend the story with one more short episode, but first of all you want to make a list of points to remember about her writing.
- Remind the children of the style-related points they have already discussed and ask for suggestions as to what you should write down. Use Shared Writing Example 1 (opposite) to guide the class.
- Read the list together and put it on display for later use.

Teacher demonstration

- Make sure children have their partially-completed Structure Charts (Copymaster C1) from Unit of work 1.
- Quickly fill in paragraphs 8 and 9 of your structure chart from Unit 1 if you have not already done so (see Shared Writing Example 2 opposite.) Explain that you are going to plan a next episode in the story and that you will start them off. They should copy what you write onto their own charts.
- *Mouse is feeling really down-hearted and dispirited after what has happened so I think we should make this obvious to the reader and start the next episode with a paragraph saying how he feels.* Using a fresh Structure Chart, fill in paragraph 10 as in Shared Writing Example 2.
- *I think that Mouse is the kind of character that would bounce back from setbacks quite quickly so I'm going to have the next paragraph with him thinking that he can't leave things like this – he needs to get some 'street cred' back. That will make the link into the next episode.* Fill in paragraph 11 as in Shared Writing Example 2.

Supported composition

- *I want you to fill in the next paragraph on your chart. Let's have Mouse deciding that that he will team up with Viola Angotti – even if it means that he will have to play at being Robin to her Batman because she is tougher than him. This will give the reader clues as to what this episode might be about.*
- Children write as above. Check two or three children's writing.
- *In the next paragraph we could have Mouse going up to Viola in the school yard at recess – that's what Americans call break or playtime - and suggesting that they team up. So as to create a bit of suspense, we won't have her answering.*
- Children write as above. Check two or three children's writing.
- *The last paragraph needs to be Viola's response. What will she do? Will she agree or will she turn him down? Maybe she'll just dump him in the trash can as her answer. You decide and fill in your chart.*
- Discuss what children have done.

Shared Writing Example: Structure Chart

1. The Author's Style

- use of American words e.g. school yard, principal
- use of exaggeration for effect and humour
- use of natural and realistic direct speech
- variety of sentence length, but short sentences often used for impact
- small descriptive details
- little use of figurative language, similes or metaphors

2.

8 (page 8)	Viola Angotti hits Mouse; Mouse is sick	• turn things round so that the victim becomes the aggressor
9 (page 9)	Viola Angotti walks off and leaves Mouse in a crumpled heap	• emphasis Viola Angotti's strength and power; add humour
10	Mouse thinks about how humiliated he feels	• to show Mouse at his lowest point
11	Mouse decides he can't leave things like this – he need to get some 'street cred' back	• show Mouse beginning to recover; make link into next episode
12	Mouse decides that he will team up with Viola Angotti – even if it means being Robin to her Batman	• give clues as to what the next episode might be about

Independent Writing

- The children write the episode. Draw their attention to the list of features of Betsy Byars' style, which they should try to emulate.
- In groups, they should discuss, proof-read and edit their own writing for clarity and correctness.

Checking Children's Learning

- How far have the children maintained consistency of character and style?

Revisiting the Objective

- Take one child's work and, with his or her permission, revise it together.

Writing objective:

T13: To record their ideas reflections and predictions about a book, e.g. through a reading log or journal

Links to sentence/word level work

S5: To understand the difference between direct and reported speech …

Text Copymasters: C10–11

Discussing the text

- Tell the children that the text they are going to read is a list of questions to help them when they are writing in their reading journals. (If you are not already using reading journals with your class, then this Unit of work could provide an introduction or starting point.)
- Read the text together.
- Point out that the four headings (Describe, Predict, Question and Reflect) sum up what journal writing should involve. They are not headings that children should actually use in their writing.
- *Would you use all four types of question in every journal entry? Why not?* (For example, some are more suited to the beginning/middle/end of a novel than others.)
- *Do you think it would be helpful for you to have this list of questions fixed in your journals?* If children agree, Copymasters C10 and C11 can be used for this.

Shared Writing

Teacher scribing

- Clip the acetate sheet to Resource Book page 10.
- Go through the questions and use the acetate to annotate a) anything which children think needs explaining and b) any questions which children think need to be developed or added to. Then do the same with page 11.

Teacher Demonstration

- Explain to the children that you are going to write a journal entry for the Betsy Byars extract which they have been working with for the last two units. *This is actually an extract from the middle of a novel but we'll pretend it is the beginning of the novel and that this is the first journal entry.*
- Tell the children that you are going to start off the entry.
- Write Shared Writing Example 1 opposite, modelling how one reads what has been written so far before continuing. The end of the second sentence is a good point to do this.
- All together, read what you have written.
- Refer to the questions in the first section of the Resource Book text ('Describe', page 10). Ask the children which ones you have covered in your writing so far.

Shared Writing Examples

1. This is a humorous story set in present day America. It is told in the third person but from the point of view of Mouse, the main character.

(Pause and read what you have written so far before continuing.)

We don't know why the boy has this nickname – it might be because he is small for his age, or perhaps he is quite timid.

2. It could be either because, in this chapter, when the boys decide to put the girls in the trash cans, Mouse ends up cornering the powerful Viola Angotti, but without help he can do nothing. Viola says that no one is putting her into a trash can and she hits Mouse – who ends up in a crumpled heap.

3. Why did Mouse and Viola behave in the way that they did?
Did Mouse deserve what happened to him?
Is the author trying to say anything to me?
How does the mood of the 'chapter' change?
What do I think about the way the episode ends?
Is there anything special about the way the author uses language?

Supported composition
- Tell the children that the next part of the journal entry will answer the question 'What is this "chapter" about?' They should use their whiteboards to summarise what happens in the chapter in no more than four sentences. While they are writing, you should write the questions in Shared Writing Example 3 above on a separate sheet of paper or on the board.
- Share some of the children's summaries and select one (or use Shared Writing Example 2) to continue your journal entry. Point out how you have linked the two pieces.
- Show the children the questions you have written (Shared Writing Example 3) and discuss them briefly.

Independent Writing
- Children should use the questions to complete the journal entry.
- Discuss and compare the writing within the group. Select one to share with the whole class.

Checking Children's Learning
- Do the children understand the nature of journal writing?
- Are they able to use questions to guide their writing?

Revisiting the Objective
- Draft a journal entry for a book currently being read by the class using questions from the Resource Book to guide the writing.

Term 1 Unit of work 4:

Write a poem conveying feelings

Writing objective

T16: To convey feelings, reflections or moods in a poem through the careful choice of words and phrases

Links to sentence/word level work

S3: To discuss, proof-read and edit their own writing for clarity and correctness …

Text Copymasters: C12–13

Discussing the text

- Read together the poem 'Evacuee' by Edith Pickthall.
- Check that the children understand the more challenging words, e.g. sordid, limpidly, abject (meaning miserable or wretched) and sough (meaning a sigh or murmur, and can be pronounced to rhyme with either rough or how)
- *What do you think of the poem?*
- *Why is the boy afraid?*
- *How does the poet portray the boy's feelings?*
- *What is the meaning of 'his case of mean necessities'?*
- *Which life does the boy think is better? Does the poet agree? How do you know?*
- *What is the rhyming scheme of the poem? How many syllables are there in most lines?*

Shared Writing

Teacher demonstration

- Tell the children that they are going to finish writing a poem about feelings which you will start. It will use the same structure as 'Evacuee'.
- *I'm going to concentrate on feelings of fear in my poem and I'm going to start like this …* Write the first line of Shared Writing Example 1. *'Fight' would be a good word to rhyme with 'night' so I'll write this for my next line …* Write the second line then read what you have written so far. *I want to show how fear is affecting her … when we are afraid we get all tensed up and perhaps clench our fists so I'm going to say …* Write the third line … *and I'll finish off by showing her starting to cry.* Write the fourth line.
- Ask the children to read what you have written so you can hear how it sounds.
- *I'm not happy with some of the word choices I've made so I'm going to make two or three changes …* (See Shared Writing Example 2.) *'Poised' doesn't make her sound frightened enough so I'll change that to 'Hunched' … I think I'd be better with a semi-colon at the end of the second line because that will make more of a break in this long sentence. 'Thin chilly fingers' doesn't sound quite right – perhaps it's something to do with the i sound being repeated or perhaps it's just not strong enough – so I'll put 'cold' instead and make 'curled' into 'curling' to give me 10 syllables in the line.*
- Read the revised poem together.

Shared Writing Example

1.   Poised at the top of the stairway at night,
       From the sounds below it could be a fight,
       With her thin chilly fingers curled in fear,
       Her dark eyes shine with the trace of a tear.

2.   ~~Poised~~ Hunched at the top of the stairway at night,
       From the sounds below it could be a fight;
       With her thin ~~chilly~~ cold fingers ~~curled~~ curling in fear,
       Her dark eyes shine with the trace of a tear

3.   A small girl sitting at the top of the stairs having been woken
       up: is it her parents arguing? a fight on television? her
       boisterous older brothers/sisters?
       – A woman about to go into her flat
       – A teenager hiding from some girls who are bullying her

Teacher scribing

- *I've deliberately written my poem so that we are not yet clear as to what is happening. What do you think is going on? Who is the female?*
- Take and list suggestions from the children. (See examples in Shared Writing Example 3 above.)
- Discuss these possibilities; what effect might each have on the female's feelings? Will they change?

Independent Writing

- Ask children to choose the scenario which most appeals to them. They should then draft their own poem – using your initial four lines if they wish.
- In pairs or groups, the children should listen to someone else reading their poems to see how they sound and then discuss, proof-read and edit their own writing.

Checking Children's Learning

- Have the children maintained the rhyming scheme and number of syllables per line in their poems?
- Have they made careful and considered word choices? *Why did you choose to use that word?*

Revisiting the Objective

- Write extra lines for Edith Pickthall's poem – perhaps having the person with whom the boy was staying finding and comforting him until his fears abate. For example, you could start children off with the lines:
      Then in the distance a figure appears,
      A shape distorted by glistening tears;

Term 1 Unit of work 5:

Write metaphors

Writing objective

T17: To write metaphors from original ideas or similes

Text Copymasters: C14–15

Discussing the text

- Tell children they are going to read some examples of metaphors.
- *Who can explain what a metaphor is? (Where a writer describes something as if it was something else.)*
- *Why do we use metaphors in writing?* (e.g. it makes descriptions more powerful and imaginative.)
- Read together the examples on page 14.
- *Some of these metaphors use personification; can anyone explain what that means?* (Personification is a form of metaphor where a writer describes a non-human thing as if it were human.)
- Identify the examples which use personification.
- Ask individuals to tell you which metaphor they think works particularly well or which conjures up a strong image in their heads.

Shared Writing

Teacher demonstration

- Show children Resource Book page 15 (Making up Metaphors) and tell them that you are going to make up metaphors for each of these things and that you will start them off.
- *The wind can be anything from a little breeze to a strong gale. I'm going to describe a breeze.* Write Shared Writing Example 1 (opposite). *Why is this a metaphor?*
- Write Shared Writing Example 2. *What kind of building could I be describing here? Is it a pleasant and inviting one? Why?*
- Write Shared Writing Example 3. *What two things tell you that I'm not describing a tree in summer?*
- Write Shared Writing Example 4. *Why is this a metaphor?*
- *Which of my metaphors use personification?*

Teacher scribing

- Tell the children that you will give them a minute to think of a metaphor which could be used to describe any one of the four things on page 15.
- Take suggestions, scribe two or three in each box. Read them together. Discuss which, if any, involve personification.
- Add any other examples or amendments that arise spontaneously.

Supported composition

- Give out copies of Copymaster C15.
- Ask the children to write a metaphor about the wind. If they have problems thinking of one, they can adapt one that has already been used.
- Share some of the examples. If children particularly like anyone else's metaphors they should add them to their own sheet.
- Repeat for the other three things.

Shared Writing Example: Making up Metaphors

1. The wind   The breeze ruffled his hair with playful fingers.

2. A building   It was waiting to swallow me up.

3. A tree   A white cloak of snow covered the naked branches.

4. An evil person   His eyes were deep pools of wickedness.

5. An Autumn Day
City Buildings
Zoltar the Terrible

Independent Writing

- Write the three titles in Shared Writing Example 5 on the board for the children to see. They should choose one and write a short description. Point out that their descriptions should include metaphors but not consist of a string of them one after the other! Fast writers should choose a second one to do.
- Discuss and compare the writing within the group. Select one to share with the whole class.

Checking Children's Learning

- Share some of the children's descriptions in the plenary session.
- Have they included metaphors in their descriptions? Are there any examples of personification?
- Can children explain what 'metaphor' and 'personification' mean?
- Do they understand their purpose?

Revisiting the Objective

- Write metaphors with the class to describe the following:
  - the sea
  - an animal, e.g. a black cat
  - an emotion, e.g. anger or jealousy
- Write a metaphor poem about one of the above.

Annotate a playscript

Writing objective

T19: To annotate a section of playscript as a preparation for performance, taking into account pace, movement, gesture and delivery of lines and the needs of the audience

Text Copymasters: C16–20

Discussing the text

- Explain to the class that they are going to read an extract from a play entitled 'Theseus and the Minotaur'. It comes from the *Pelican Big Book* title of that name (Longman), which children may already have met. If not, establish that they have some idea of the story of Theseus and the Minotaur. They need to know that Ariadne is the daughter of the king who has the labyrinth in his palace and that each year the King of Athens has to send a group of young men and women to be sacrificed. Theseus, his son, has gone with them, vowing to kill the Minotaur, Asterion.
- Establish that the children understand what the labyrinth is like.
- Read the extract from Act 3: Inside the Labyrinth – either in unison or with groups taking the five parts and you reading the stage directions.
- What do the children think will happen next?

Shared Writing

Teacher demonstration

- Give children copies of Copymasters C16–C20. Have spare sets available for the independent writing. Clip the acetate to page 16 of the Resource Book.
- Explain that the class are going to perform the extract and make notes on the playscript in order to help with performance.
- Read Periboea's speech. *I think it's the middle of the night and Theseus is sleeping so Ariadne would have to wake him up before she speaks so I'm going to add a couple of things here* (See Shared Writing Example opposite).
- *Ariadne would be excited about the fact that she is going to help Theseus and save his life so she would speak quite quickly and I think she would pause before she says 'Look what I've brought'* … annotate as in the Shared Writing Example.
- *The person playing Ariadne would have to hold the string out to Theseus who would then take it so I'll note that down* … (Shared Writing Example.)
- *What do you think that Theseus would do and think at this point? Remember he's got to try and kill this powerful monster and there is this woman giving him a ball of string! Yes, I think he'd look at her as if she was stupid and sound as if he thought it, too.* Annotate as in the Shared Writing Example.
- *I think Ariadne would respond quite firmly and stress that the string is enchanted* … Annotate as in the Shared Writing Example.

Teacher scribing

- *Read through what I've done and see if there is anything else you think I ought to add.*
- Discuss and scribe any suggestions.

Act 3: **Inside the Labyrinth**

Periboea (as narrator)

That night, Ariadne went to see

Theseus ... ——————— *asleep on bench or floor*

(Ariadne shakes his arm to wake him up.)

Ariadne **Theseus, I want to help**

you kill that dreadful

pause

monster. **Look what**

I've brought. *(holds out ball of string, Theseus takes it.)*

excited so speaks quickly

1 Looks at ball of string —

Theseus **A ball of string? What**

use is that?

2 Looks at her then speaks as if she is stupid

stress this

Ariadne **It is enchanted string.**

Tie it to the doorpost

of the Labyrinth.

speaks firmly

- Give the children two or three minutes to write your annotations on their own copies of Copymaster C16.

Supported composition

- In pairs, children should then annotate the next page of their copymasters (C17). They should think about how Ariadne will speak, what Theseus will be doing while she is speaking, how Theseus will reply. Will either of them use any gestures?
- Compare and discuss annotations.

Independent Writing

- Working individually within their groups, children should annotate the rest of the extract. They should not add anything about the actual fight.
- Each group should then compare and discuss individual annotations and reach consensus. Group members should end up with the same annotations ready for later performance. Some children may need fresh copymasters.
- Collect and keep the annotated copymasters (make sure that the children have put their names on them) for use in Unit of work 8.

Checking Children's Learning

- Have the children understood the purpose of the annotation?
- Have they differentiated between what characters are doing and how they are speaking?

Revisiting the Objective

- Use another page from the extract to annotate as a class.

Writing objective

T18: To write own playscript, applying conventions learned from reading; include production notes

Links to sentence/word level work

S6: To understand the need for punctuation as an aid to the reader

Text Copymasters: C16–21

Discussing the text

- Depending on how recently the children have completed Unit of work 6, either re-read or recap on the extract 'Inside the Labyrinth' (pages 16 to 20).
- Discuss what the children think will happen next.

Shared Writing

Session 1
Teacher demonstration

- Have the acetate clipped to page 21 of the Resource Book (What will happen next?).
- Tell the children that they are going to write the next section of the play but that first of all you are going to plan it together. Read through page 21 together.
- Explain that the section of the scene to be written will finish at the point where Theseus, Ariadne, Hermus and Periboea are about to free their companions ready to board the ship back to Athens.
- *The extract finishes at the point where Asterion says 'Get ready to die!' and Theseus is moving closer to the Minotaur. He will obviously say something back again. It says that in the first bullet point but I'm just going to add a bit to remind us what is going on …* (See the first bullet point in the Shared Writing Example. Do not add the annotation ('D' for 'dialogue') until later.
- *I think there would probably be some shouting of insults and taunting each other at this stage before they start to fight so I'm going to write …* (second bullet point in the Shared Writing Example.)
- *Now they will actually start to fight …* (third bullet point in the Shared Writing Example opposite.)

Supported composition

- Give the children a verbal outline of how the rest of the scene might proceed using the Shared Writing Example.
- Give them five minutes to outline the rest of the scene in seven or eight bullet points at most. They should work in pairs and use their whiteboards.
- Take suggestions, select and scribe.

Teacher scribing

- Refer to the bottom part of the page you are using (Resource Book page 21) and explain that you are going to annotate the bullet points (as in the Shared Writing Example opposite). Remind children that they will need a balance of dialogue (D), narration (N) and stage directions (SD) when thinking how each part can be done.
- Go through each bullet point taking suggestions for annotation.

Shared Writing Example

- Theseus responds to what Asterion has said ('Get ready to die!') as he gets closer to the Minotaur (**D**)

- Still apart, they taunt each other (**D**) (**SD**)

- Asterion makes a grab for Theseus but he dodges out of the way (**N**)

- Asterion stumbles, Theseus takes his chance and jumps on Asterion (**N**)

- Asterion throws him to the ground (**D**) (**SD**) and Theseus is dazed (**N**)

- Asterion is about to finish him off (**D**)

- Ariadne (who has followed Theseus using the string) (**N**) shouts a warning to Theseus, (**D**) picks up a rock and hurls it at Asterion to distract him (**SD**)

- Theseus grabs Asterion from behind and strangles him (**N**)

- Ariadne checks that Theseus is all right (**D**)

- They set off to free Theseus' companions (**D**)

Independent Writing

Session 2

- Remind children about the features of playscripts using Copymaster C2.
- As a group, the children should write the rest of the scene using the plan from the Shared Writing to guide them.
- On completion, each group should go through their script checking for flow and how well it reads. They should pay particular attention to punctuation as an aid to the reader.
- Each group should then annotate the script for performance. Give them their annotated copymasters from Unit 6 to help with this.
- Give the children time before the next Unit to practise reading their scripts. They must NOT rehearse a performance. This is important!

Checking Children's Learning

- Have the children set out their playscripts correctly?
- Is there a balance between dialogue, narration and stage directions?
- Is there evidence of thoughtful use of punctuation?

Revisiting the Objective

- Plan and write a different version of the fight between Theseus and Asterion.

Evaluate the playscript

Writing objective

T20: To evaluate the script and the performance for their dramatic interest and impact

Text Copymasters: C16–21

NB You will probably need an extended literacy hour for this lesson.

Discussing the text

- Have the questions in the Shared Writing Example already written out for children to see as a class. Leave space for further questions to be added under each section.
- Tell children that they are going to perform their Theseus scripts and that they will be evaluating both the performances and the scripts.
- Explain that this list of questions will help their evaluation and then read through the questions.

Shared Writing

Teacher scribing

- Tell the children that you want them to think about whether there are any other questions which should be added to the list. *Are there any more questions for the audience? Are there any more questions for the cast?* Give them a minute or two to discuss this in pairs.
- Take suggestions and scribe.
- Read through all the questions together.

Shared Writing Example

Evaluating the script and performance

Questions for the Audience:

- Could you hear what everyone was saying?
- Did they sound natural?
- Did the performance hold your interest?
- Did anyone behave stupidly during the fight scene?

Questions for the Cast:

- Did the audience concentrate and listen properly?
- How helpful were your stage directions?
- How helpful were your annotations for performance?
- Was there anything you should have written in but didn't?
- How easy is it to perform a script when you have to read from it?

**Groups should now take it in turns to perform their scripts.
The audience may make notes if they wish.**

Checking Children's Learning

- Either after each group's performance or at the end, go through the list of questions to help guide the evaluation and discussion. If you do the evaluation at the end of all the performances, you may find it helpful to tell each group that after their performance and while the next group is getting ready, they will have a minute to discuss or jot down any thoughts they have about their performance and script. The audience can do the same.
- *What have you learned about:*
  - *annotating playscripts to help prepare for performance?*
  - *how to evaluate a play performance?*
  - *why actors need to learn their lines by heart?*

Independent Writing

- Members of each group should work together to write a brief account of their performance and their evaluation of both script and performance.
- Write a review of your group's performance and script as if you were a theatre critic.

Revisiting the Objective

- Write an evaluation as a class of the success of the performances and playscripts.

Writing objective

T1: To identify and classify the features of myths

Links to sentence/word level work

S5: To use punctuation effectively to signpost meaning in longer and more complex sentences

Text Copymasters: C22–27

Discussing the text

- Tell the children that they are going to read a retelling of a Native American story. Do not say that it is a myth at this stage.
- Read 'Tee-rah-wah's Gift' together and allow brief comments/responses.
- Give children copies of Copymaster C3, Ancient Stories. (They can share in twos or threes.) Explain that this is a summary of the features of three different kinds of ancient story: myths, legends and folktales. The chart shows their similarities and differences.
- Ask children to read through the sheet and use it to discuss and decide the genre of 'Tee-rah-wah's Gift'. While they are doing this, write 'Tee-rah-wah's Gift' is a _____ because:' on your paper.

Shared Writing

Teacher scribing

- Collect up the copymasters (C3) and ask the children to identify the story genre.
- Draw their attention to what you have written and fill in 'myth'.
- Ask for suggestions as to what you should write as supporting evidence. (See the Shared Writing Example 1 opposite for guidance)

Supported composition

- Children should work in pairs to write on their whiteboards the reasons why the story is not a legend.
- Take suggestions and scribe. (See the Shared Writing Example 2 for guidance.)
- Children should now write the reasons why the story is not a folktale.
- Take suggestions and scribe. (See the Shared Writing Example 3 for guidance.)
- Put the paper to one side – it will be needed later.

Discussing the Text

- Clip on the acetate and re-read Resource Book page 22. Ask children to identify how many sentences are used on this page.
- *Look at the first sentence. Why are there commas after 'ago' and 'America'?* (to mark or separate the subordinate clause) *How do we know this is a subordinate clause?* (It cannot stand alone as a sentence.)
- Ask the children to identify subordinate clauses in the other two sentences. Underline them.
- *Why has the author used ellipsis in the last sentence?*

- *Could we change the order of clauses in this sentence? What happens to the punctuation if we put the main clause, 'Kenu's leg slowly improved' at the beginning of the sentence. Why didn't the author do this?* (Because it might suggest that the Medicine Man had something to do with Kenu's mother dying; it interferes with the contrast of Kenu getting better but his mother dying.)
- Experiment with making changes to the punctuation and order, e.g. 'One night, his mother became ill. Running to fetch help, Kenu fell – and broke his leg.' Are there advantages or disadvantages to making these changes?

Shared Writing Example

'Tee-rah-wah's Gift' is a myth because:

- it explains how the Plains Indians came to have horses and why these horses are smaller
- it features a god, Tee-rah-wah, who helps humans by giving them something they need and controls the main character, Kenu, in order to do this

It is not a legend because:

- it does not feature a human hero or present ideals of virtue and bravery
- the main character and plot cannot be based on a real person or event

It is not a folktale because:

- the story is not about good triumphing over evil
- it does not contain the standard features of folktales

Independent Writing

- Place the Shared Writing Example where lower ability children can see it and give out Copymaster C3 to the class to support their writing.
- Children should write a one paragraph summary of the story and then two or three paragraphs about the genre, giving reasons for the identification. It should be written in continuous prose and not as bullet points.

Checking Children's Learning

- Have the children used complex sentences in their writing?
- Are they appropriately punctuated?
- Can the children tell you the similarities and differences between myths, legends and folktales?

Revisiting the Objective

- Use Resource Book page 24 to examine complex sentences and their punctuation.

Term 1 Unit of work 10:

Write a myth

Resource Book pages 22–27

Writing objective

T11: To write own versions of legends, myths and fables, using structures and themes identified in reading

Text Copymasters: C22–27

Discussing the text

- Tell the children that you want to look at 'Tee-rah-wah's Gift' in more detail and that there are some things in the story which readers have to work out for themselves.
- *Why does Kenu's mother have to die?* Point out that there has to be a reason for Kenu being left alone in the village otherwise the story would not work – hence the father being dead already, the need for the mother to die and the broken leg as a reason to keep the boy in the village.
- *Why does Tee-rah-wah want to give the tribe horses?* (Because they have to hunt buffalo on foot.)
- *Why do there need to be two horses and not one?*
- *Do you think the story would be better if the author had given us more detail? Are there things you would have liked to know more about?*

Shared Writing

Teacher demonstration

- Tell children that they are going to write their own longer versions of this myth and that you want to identify the parts which could be expanded.
- Write the heading as in the Shared Writing Example ('Places where the story could be expanded …'). Read from 'One night' to '… his mother died' on page 22 of the Resource Book.
- *I think that we could have a lot more detail than is given in these two sentences. First of all about Kenu's mother … did she suddenly become ill or had she been poorly and now she is worse? Was it the middle of the night? Did she wake her son or did Kenu hear her moaning, for example? How did he feel? Was he in a panic?* Write the first bullet point of the Shared Writing Example.
- *Now what about Kenu breaking his leg? I think there are some questions that need to be answered here as well.* Write the second bullet point of the Shared Writing Example.

Teacher scribing

- *Do you think more needs to be said about Kenu's mother dying? What questions does the story leave unanswered for us?*
- Scribe children's questions along the lines of the third bullet point of the Shared Writing Example.
- Read the first three lines of page 23 down to '… the rest of the tribe'; *I think there are lots of questions here …* Prompt as per the fourth bullet point of the Shared Writing Example and scribe children's suggestions.
- Continue through the rest of the story, allowing children to identify the parts which could be expanded and scribing the questions needing to be addressed.

Shared Writing Example

Places where the story could be expanded and have more detail:

- **Kenu's mother becoming ill:** had she been poorly? Did she wake him up? How did he feel?

- **Kenu breaking his leg:** what happened? How did he fall? Who found him? What happened then?

- **His mother dying:** how did Kenu feel? When did this happen? the same night? some weeks later?

- **Spring:** who told Kenu that he could not go with the tribe? the Chief? What would he have said? Would Kenu have argued? Would the Chief have promised Kenu that he could go the following year? Would he have said that Kenu was old enough to care for himself and also to look after the village for the tribe while they were away?

Independent Writing

- The children should write their own versions of the myth using the questions devised during the Shared Writing as prompts for where they should include additional detail. You may wish to provide one set of Text Copymasters C22–27 per table in case children want to refer to the original story. You could restrict this and provide the extra support for your less able children only.
- Points to stress:
  - The children should write the story in their own way and in their own words
  - When it comes to adding to the original version, the questions are to remind them of things they might think about including. They are not to be answered one by one
- **NOTE: the children's work will be needed for Unit of work 13.**

Checking Children's Learning

- Have the children included all the essential elements of the story?
- Have they expanded the original and added more detail and description?

Revisiting the Objective

- Plan the story from Tee-rah-wah's point of view, i.e. with the god as onlooker and observer as well as instigator.

Term 2 Unit of work 11:

Adapt writing for a different audience

Resource Book pages 22–27

Writing objective

T13: To review and edit writing to produce a final form, matched to the needs of an identified reader

Links to sentence/word level work

S3: To understand how writing can be adapted for different audiences and purposes, e.g. by changing vocabulary and sentence structures

Text Copymasters: C22-27

Discussing the text

- Explain that myths can be written in different versions in order to appeal to different age ranges. If you wish, you can tell children that a version of 'Tee-rah-wah's Gift' was the first book which Wendy Body ever had published. It was originally written for seven year olds and she shortened it and adapted the language for this version.
- Ask the class if they agree that this story would appeal to younger children.

Shared Writing

Teacher demonstration

- Explain to the class that they are going to adapt the story 'Tee-rah-wah's Gift' to make it suitable for younger children to read. *This means that the language will need to be changed to make it suitable for children who can't read as well as you. They wouldn't be able to manage complex sentences so we will need to change them. They wouldn't know some of the words either. We need to make the story as simple as we can. Breaking it into shorter paragraphs will also help.*
- You can either annotate the text using the acetate or rewrite it a section at a time.
- Read the first sentence of the story on Resource Book page 22. *This sentence is much too complicated. Younger children won't understand about buffalo roaming the grasslands of America ... I also think we need to say that Kenu's father died when he was a baby. His mother is about to die as well and we don't want these younger children getting too upset thinking that his mum and dad have died one after the other. We could change it like this ...* Annotate or write the first paragraph as in Shared Writing Example 1a opposite. Read it back.
- Repeat with Shared Writing Example 2 and 2a. Point out the need for greater explanation here.
- Repeat with Shared Writing Example 3 and 3a. Explain that you are adding more detail to prepare the younger reader for the fact that Kenu is about to be left behind when the tribe go hunting.
- Read back what has been written so far. *How does it sound? Are we happy with it?*

Shared Writing Examples

1. *Long, long ago, when the buffalo roamed the grasslands of America, Kenu lived alone with his mother for his father had been killed while hunting.*

1a. Long, long ago, an Indian boy called Kenu lived with his mother. His father died when Kenu was a baby. He had been killed when he was out hunting.

2. *One night, his mother became ill; Kenu, running to fetch help, fell and broke his leg.*

2a. One night, Kenu's mother became ill. He knew he must get help. He ran out of the hut but it was dark and he could not see. Kenu fell and broke his leg.

3. *With the help of Medicine Man and members of the tribe, Kenu's leg slowly improved … but, sadly, his mother died.*

3a. The people of the tribe looked after Kenu and his mother. But Kenu's mother was very ill and she died. Kenu was very sad. Slowly his leg got better. Kenu could look after himself but he could not walk a long way.

4. *When Spring came, Kenu was unable to set out on the long trek to hunt buffalo with the rest of the tribe;*

4a. Spring came and it was time for the tribe to go off and hunt for buffalo. But Kenu could not go with them. It was too far for him to walk. The Chief said, "Stay here and look after the village, Kenu. You can come with us next year when your leg is stronger."

Teacher scribing

*   Read the first part of the sentence at the start of page 23 as in Shared Writing Example 4. *How are we going to simplify this and make it easier to understand? Do we want to say why Kenu can't go and that it is the Chief who tells him he must stay behind?* Give children a minute to discuss this in pairs.
*   Take suggestions, select and scribe.
*   Finish the rest of page 23. It needs only small changes.

Independent Writing *(more than one session)*

*   Children should work in groups to simplify the rest of the story using Text Copymasters C24–27.
*   When they are happy with their changes, they should produce a final version which they can take and read with younger children in the school.

Checking Children's Learning

*   Discuss how easy or difficult children found the task of adaptation.
*   How did the story go down with younger children? Would they make further changes as a result?

Revisiting the Objective

*   Compare the second half of one group's version with the original. Establish why the changes were made.

Term 2 Unit of work 12:

Write an extension to the poem

Writing objective

T12: To use the structures of poems read to write extensions based on these, e.g. additional verses or substituting own words and ideas

Text Copymasters: C28–30

Discussing the text

- 'Overheard on a Saltmarsh' (pages 28 to 30) is a famous poem by Harold Monro, which you may have already used with the children. It may not be necessary, therefore, to cover all the following.
- Read the poem together, with half the class reading the goblin's lines and the other half reading the nymph's.
- *How would you describe this poem? Does it appeal to you? Why?*
- *What is a nymph?* (a young goddess living in the sea, rivers or woods)
- *Does the poem have a recognisable form or structure? Does it rhyme at all?*

Shared Writing

Teacher scribing

- Tell the children that they are going to write a poem based on the one they have just read, using the same pattern and structure. Have Monro's poem on view.
- *I want our poem to be called 'Overheard in a Wood'. It will be a conversation between a goblin and a traveller in the woods. The traveller has a sword made of gold and steel, which the goblin wants.*
- *What shall I write for the first line? ... Yes, 'Traveller, traveller, what is your sword?'* (Shared Writing Example 1, opposite.)
- *Now what shall I write?*
- Continue scribing Shared Writing Example 1.
- *What can we put instead of 'Then I will howl all night in the reeds, Lie in the mud and howl for them.'?*
- Take suggestions and scribe. (See Shared Writing Example 2.)

Teacher demonstration

- *I'll do the next lines for you because I want to give you a lead in to the rest of our poem. I want to show that the goblin has some plan in mind.*
- Scribe Shared Writing Example 3. *Have I used the same structure as in the original poem?*
- Read what has been read so far with half the class reading the goblin's lines and half reading the traveller's.

Teacher scribing

- Tell children that they are going to continue the poem themselves but that you want to discuss possibilities with them first.
- *Why might the goblin want the sword? What is his plan?*
- List children's suggestions. Include those in Shared Writing Example 4.

Overheard in a Wood

1. Traveller, traveller, what is your sword?
    Gold and steel, goblin. Why do you stare at it?
    Give it me.
    No.
    Give it me. Give it me.
    No.

2. Then I will howl all night in the woods,
    Run through the trees and howl for it.
    Goblin, why do you want it so?

3. The gold shines like the sun in the sky,
    I want to feel its warmth in my hand,
    The steel is sharp like a falcon's cry
    And I need it for what I have planned.

4. Ideas for continuation:
    –   traveller stole sword from a wizard, goblin has been sent to get
        it back
    –   goblin knows that traveller is King Arthur in disguise and he
        wants the famous sword
    –   goblin needs a weapon to kill the dragon which has taken his
        cave

Independent Writing

*   The children should decide on their reason for the goblin wanting the sword
    and whether or not the traveller will part with it. They should then complete
    the poem. It does not matter how long their poems are, provided that they
    keep to the conversation format.
*   When they are happy with their drafts, the children should make a fair copy of
    the complete poem.

Checking Children's Learning

*   Share some of the poems. Discuss how children tackled the writing, why they
    chose certain words/phrases/lines and what they think of their work.

Revisiting the Objective

*   Choose one of the continuation ideas that was not widely used and write a
    version of the poem together.

Writing objective

T13: To review and edit writing to produce a final form, matched to the needs of an identified reader

Links to sentence/word level work

S5: To use punctuation effectively to signpost meaning in longer and more complex sentences

Text Copymasters: C31–34

Discussing the text

- Tell the children that the texts they are going to read in this unit of work are to give them help in revising and editing their writing.

Session 1

- *Look at pages 32 and 33 of the Resource Book.*
  You know that we have something called Grammar, which describes how language works? Well there is also something called Story Grammar, which describes how stories work. All stories have the same basic elements and that is what is described here …
- Read pages 32 and 33 to the class.
- *So: all stories have settings, main and secondary characters and are told in the first or third person. You knew that already, didn't you? But stories also have this structure to them: an opening or introduction, an initiating event – something which starts everything off – a response to the initiating event and then in turn a reaction to that. The action–reaction pattern gets repeated until we reach the climax or the high point of the story. Then we get the resolution when things are sorted out. Let's see if we can check this out against a story we read last term …*
- Turn back to page 2 in the Resource Book to the extract called 'Viola Angotti' to look at the illustrations and refresh children's memories. Ask them about setting, characters and first or third person narrative.

Shared Writing

Teacher demonstration

- Have the chart shared Writing Example (see opposite) already prepared with the first two columns filled in and turn back to pages 32 and 33 in the Resource Book.
- Explain what you have written on the chart so far and ask the class to help you fill in the rest.

Teacher scribing

- Go through the chart, stopping after each Content summary to identify the Story Structure label in column 3. Guide the children using the Shared Writing Example if necessary.
- Pose questions for consolidation, e.g. *What have we said is the high point of the story? How are the initiating event and the resolution linked? How many times does the action–reaction pattern occur?*

Shared Writing Example

Paragraph	Content	Story Structure
1 (page 2)	the boys decide to put the girls in the trash cans	Introduction and initiating event
2 (pages 2–3)	Mouse chases the girls and catches Viola Angotti	Response to initiating event
3 & 4 (page 4)	Mouse realises he'll need help and shouts	Action
4 & 5 (pages 4–5)	no one comes to help Mouse	Reaction
6 (page 6)	Viola Angotti stands up to Mouse	Action
7 (page 8)	Mouse shouts for help again	Reaction
8 (page 8)	Viola Angotti hits Mouse	Climax
8 & 9 (pages 8–9)	Viola Angotti walks off; Mouse has learned that no one will ever put Viola Angotti in a trash can	Resolution

Independent Writing

- Children work in pairs to analyse a recent story they have written.

Discussing the Text

Session 2

- Go through the advice on revising writing on pages 34 and 35 of the Resource Book.
- Make sure that the children understand all the statements.

Supported composition

- Clip the acetate over page 35. Ask the children if there is anything else that they think ought to be included (e.g. 'You can change the language to make it suitable for your audience.') and add to the list accordingly.

Independent Writing

- Give children copies of Copymasters C31–34. (You may want the children to keep these in their folders or books to refer to when revising in the future.) Ensure they have the myths they wrote in Unit 10.
- Children should use the copymaster guidance to help them make revisions to their writing in Unit 10 ('Write a myth').

Checking Children's Learning

- Ask children what they should look for when revising their writing.

Revisiting the Objective

- Display examples of first drafts and final versions of the myths. Discuss the changes the writers have made.

Writing objective

T14: To make notes of story outline as preparation for oral storytelling

Links to sentence/word level work

S6: To be aware of the differences between spoken and written language ...

Text Copymasters: C35–36

Discussing the text

- Ask children to read through the poem 'Counting the Stars' silently before you read it aloud all together.
- *What do you think of the poem?*
- *Do you think the way the poet has described the stars is effective? Why?*
- *How else could you describe stars?*
- *Look at the moral at the end. What kind of story does this remind you of?*
- Close the book and ask if anyone can tell the story.
- Praise the volunteer and say that it was a really good effort considering there was no time to prepare.
- Tell children that they are going to turn this poem into a story but that good storytelling involves preparation.

Shared Writing

Teacher demonstration

- *The poem is like the bare bones of a story; we need to put some flesh on them by adding some extra details. What we are going to do is make some notes which will remind us of what to say when we are telling the story. I'll start you off.*
- *This is how I might start my story ... There was once a man called John who lived in a small cottage in the country. During the summer it would get very hot inside the cottage so John used to go out walking whenever he could ... I only need to write enough down to remind me ...* Write the first bullet point of the Shared Writing Example.
- *I'm not going to tell the next part of my story, I'm just going to write the notes ...* Write the rest of the Shared Writing Example.
- *Let's see if my notes are good enough ... Who would like to carry on the story using what I have written?*
- Ask the children if they think any changes need to be made.

Teacher scribing

- Ask for suggestions as to how the story might continue – i.e. get John noticing the stars and what they look like, starting to count them (why?) and get him into the wood.
- Ask how you would translate these into notes and scribe.

Independent Writing

- Give out Text Copymasters C35–36 (one per group). Ask the children to work as a group to make notes for their own version of the story. They do not have to use the ideas or notes from the Shared Writing.
- When they have finished their notes, they should decide which group member will tell which part of the story aloud and have a practice run.
- Groups should then take it in turns to tell their story to the class and show their notes when they have finished. It is obviously desirable to tape record the story-telling if possible so that children can hear for themselves how it went.
- Point out that another way to describe the telling of a story aloud is 'oral storytelling'.

Checking Children's Learning

- How did the children sound? Did they sound as if they were actually telling a story rather than simply reporting what a story was about?
- How did children use the notes – were they simply reading from them or did they genuinely use them for reference only?
- How detailed were the notes? Too much or too little detail?
- What is each group's assessment of their own notes?
- What did the rest of the class notice in terms of differences between spoken and written language? For example: Could they hear sentence boundaries? Was there much descriptive language? Were there any ums and ahs because people were speaking rather than reading?

Revisiting the Objective

- Any narrative poem can be the basis for a similar exercise. You will find some in the Pelican Big Book 'Story Poems' published by Longman.
- Ask groups to plot and note a story. Then swap notes to tell another group's story.

Writing objective
T8: To record predictions, questions, reflections while reading

Discussing the text, Shared and Independent Writing

- The format of this unit is different. Children should not see the text in the Resource Book during this session. Instead you should read aloud the text in the Text to Read Aloud box (opposite) to the class.
- Tell the children that you are going to read an extract from a story to them and that the extract is called 'Something wrong with the stove?'
- Explain that you will be stopping the reading at certain points and that you want them to write down what they are asked. They should write in sentences or notes – not single words because they will need to make sense of their answers and predictions later.
- Stress that it is important that no one says anything about what they are thinking or predicting. If they have any questions about something or there is something they are not sure about, they should write that down as well.
- Children should use paper or their notebooks and not whiteboards. (They need to write a reasonable amount and you also don't want them to make surreptitious changes!)
- Read the extract, stopping to give the instructions in italics. Don't allow discussion.
- After the reading, discuss what the children have written.

Teacher demonstration and Independent writing

- Tell the children that they are going to use the notes they made while you were reading to write a summary of their thoughts and predictions.
- Explain that you want them to use the following framework and write it up for them.

    My predictions and thoughts about the story
    To begin with, I thought that the story might be about …
    However, I changed my mind when …
        because …
    I made these predictions …
    I was right about …
        but I was wrong about …
    I had these questions in my mind: …

Checking Children's Learning

- Share some of the summaries. Have children kept to the framework?

Revisiting the Objective

- Write a summary for the class which includes examples of different reactions and viewpoints: "Some of us thought that … but others …"

Shared Writing Example

Text to Read Aloud

1. *The title of this story is 'Something wrong with the stove?' What do you think the story might be about?*

They both knew that humans did not like dogs to go into buildings which had towers and tall narrow windows. They had no idea why, and had at first been a little hurt when told firmly to wait outside.

2. *Write down who you think the story is about or who 'they' refers to and what you think the buildings with towers and tall narrow windows are.*

But Mrs Dearly had once said: "We would love you to come in if it were allowed. And I would go in far oftener if you could." So it was obviously one of those mysterious things such as no-one – not even humans – ever being allowed to walk on certain parts of the grass in Regent's Park.

3. *Write down your guess as to what book you think this extract is from.*

"We must get them out quickly," said Pongo, "and go on with our journey." They soon found the door in the tower – which the biggest pups had pushed wide open.

4. *Write down the name of the book the extract is from and how you know.*

Because Missis had always been left outside, she disliked these curious buildings with towers and high windows; but the minute she got inside, she changed her mind. This was a wonderful place – so peaceful and, somehow, so welcoming. "But where are the pups?" she said, peering all around.
She saw lots of black patches on the moonlit floor but had quite forgotten that the pups were now black. Then she remembered and as she drew nearer to the sleeping pups, tears sprang to her eyes. "Look, look at all the puppy beds!" she cried. "What good people must live here!"
"It can't be the kind of place I thought it was," said Pongo.

5. *Write down if you have changed your mind about what the building is and write down what you think the puppy beds might be.*

He was about to wake the puppies when Missis stopped him. "Let me sit by the stove for a little while," she said. "Not too long, my dear," said Pongo.
He need not have worried. Missis only sat still for a few minutes. Then she got up, shook herself, and said brightly; "Let us start now. Things are going to be all right."
An hour or so later, just before the evening service, the Verger said to the Vicar: "I think there must be something wrong with the stove, sir."

6. *Write down why you think the Verger says there is something wrong with the stove.*

On every hassock he had found a small circular patch of soot.

Writing objective

T9: To write in the style of the author, e.g. writing on to complete a section, resolve a conflict …

Links to sentence/word level work

S7: To use connectives to link clauses within sentences and to link sentences in longer texts

Text Copymasters: C37–42

Discussing the text

- Read together the extract 'Something wrong with the stove?'
- *Why do you think the dogs are in the church? Who went in first? The pups or Pongo and Missis? How do you know?* Explain that in the book Pongo and Missis have sent the puppies to shelter from the cold in what they think, from a distance, is a barn while they mend the wheel on the cart used to carry the smallest puppy.
- *Why do you think the puppies are covered in soot?*
- *How would you describe Dodie Smith's style of writing? For example, is it lively? Does she use a lot of detailed descriptions? Does she use short, simple sentences?*
- Identify and discuss how clauses and sentences are linked, e.g. on Resource Book page 38 or on pages 40 and 41.

Shared Writing

Teacher demonstration

- Tell children that they are going to write a short piece which would go *before* the extract and which will explain why the puppies are covered in soot and why the dogs are in a church.
- *The important thing is that it must be written in such a way that we wouldn't notice any differences between your writing and Dodie Smith's writing. So to do that we need to look closely at her writing in this extract.*
- Write the heading for Shared Writing Example 1 (opposite).
- *The first thing we can say is that it's written in the third person from a dog's point of view …* Write the first bullet point in Shared Writing Example 1.
- *One thing she does is to link the dogs' present experiences to their past memories – when she talks about the church at the beginning so I'll say …* Write the second bullet point in Shared Writing Example 1.

Teacher scribing

- Ask the children what else you should add to the list.
- In addition to anything children might suggest, guide them with questions to ensure that the remaining bullet points in Shared Writing Example 1 are included.
- Go through the completed list together.

Shared Writing Examples

1. Points about the writer's style in this extract:
   - written in the third person from a dog's point of view so things described in that way (e.g. the church, Regent's Park)
   - relates present experiences to past memories
   - mainly uses quite long complex sentences
   - does not use a lot of detailed descriptions
   - examples of dashes being used instead of brackets and for addition or 'afterthoughts' to sentences
   - mainly uses 'said' for direct speech
   - uses a colon before direct speech

2. Pongo felt proud of the way he and Missis had managed to get the wheel back on the cart. They had dealt with several problems and had several good ideas on the journey so far – like getting the pups to roll in the soot.

3. – why Pongo got the puppies to roll in the soot (thoughts? dialogue?)
   – what Missis is thinking or saying as they are walking to the church (needs to explain why the pups have been sent there)
   – how they realise as they approach it that the building is not a barn

Teacher demonstration

- *Remember that our piece of writing is going explain why the puppies are covered in soot and why the dogs are in a church. Now we obviously can't tell the whole story of how they covered themselves in soot as a disguise, we have to summarise it in some way. We said that Dodie Smith relates present experiences to past memories so I think it would be a good idea to have one of the dogs remembering this.*
- Explain that you need an introductory sentence or two. *I'm going to give the reason why Pongo and Missis are not with the pups and introduce the idea of the soot …* Write Shared Writing Example 2. Mention that you are using a dash – one of the style points on the list.
- Ask children to read what you have written. *Why have I got Pongo remembering the soot and not Missis?* (Because it says in the extract that Missis had forgotten that the pups were black.)

Independent Writing

- Tell the children that you want them to finish off the writing. *You can write what you want but you will need to cover these things …* Write Shared Writing Example 3 above. Remind them of the list of points about style.

Checking Children's Learning

- With the class, take examples of children's writing; check them against the list of points about writing style. What connectives have been used?

Revisiting the Objective

- Write a preceding section as a shared composition.

Write from another character's point of view

Writing objective

T7: To write from another character's point of view, e.g. retelling an incident in letter form

Text Copymasters: C37–42

Shared writing

Teacher demonstration

- Have the Shared Writing Example (opposite) already written out.
- Tell the children that they are going to use the extract from 'One Hundred and One Dalmatians' on pages 38 to 43 of the Resource Book to write the story from another character's point of view.
- *To make it interesting, we're going to invent a new character by the name of Whisker Churchmouse. He is a mouse who was watching everything that went on inside the church and he is going to be describing it to his Great Aunt Henrietta.*
- *I've been thinking how we could start off this story and I decided to write the opening for you.*
- Show children the writing, read it to them and discuss their reactions. Ask if there is anything they want to change or add.

Teacher scribing

- *Can you guess what Whisker's mum is likely to say now? Yes, she'll suggest that he tells Great Aunt Henrietta the story about all those dogs which he told her.*
- Ask children what you could write, select and then scribe.
- Ask for suggestions for Whisker's response and scribe.

Supported composition

- *Now we need to get Whisker together with Great Aunt Henrietta. Talk about it first in pairs and then write two or three sentences which will lead in to Whisker telling his Great Aunt about what happened.*
- Ask some of the children to read out their writing. Check that all the examples lead naturally in to the start of Whisker's account.

Whisker Churchmouse lived with his parents in St Mary's Church, along with his nine younger brothers and sisters. Life was pleasant for the young mouse; there were plenty of places in which to play and several times a week there was entertainment in the form of people coming to his home to sing. There was just one thing which now made him unhappy: Great Aunt Henrietta – who lived in St Michael's Church – had come to visit for the day.

"Whisker, your dad and I need to go and find something for lunch so you will have to sit with Great Aunt Henrietta while we are gone," his mum said.

"But, Mum, I can't!" Whisker cried, "I never know what to say to her!"

Independent Writing

- Children write their version of the opening and then the conversation between Whisker and his Great Aunt. They could copy the Shared Writing opening if you wish – especially the lowest ability group.
- Some further discussion will be needed before children start their writing:
  - some description and speculation about the characters Whisker is observing should be included
  - it will make the narrative more interesting if Great Aunt Henrietta asks questions from time to time, e.g. "But why were the puppies all covered in soot?" "I don't know – perhaps they'd all climbed up into a chimney." "Ah yes, I've heard humans talking about chimneys and Father Christmas on Christmas Eve."
  - the conversation – particularly Whisker's account – should sound like someone talking
  - the children will need to include something about the dogs leaving the church even though this is not in the extract
  - Whisker should say how he felt at certain points, e.g. stifling his giggles at what the Verger said to the Vicar.

Checking Children's Learning

- Do the children's accounts work as a piece of writing in their own right?
- Does the conversation section sound natural?
- Have they included all the events of the extract?

Revisiting the Objective

- Write the Verger's account of what happened as a short article in the parish magazine. He can include someone's eye-witness account of a huge number of dogs leaving the church.

Writing objective

T10: To write discursively about a novel or story, e.g. to describe, explain or comment on it

Links to sentence/word level work

S4: To use punctuation marks accurately in complex sentences

Text Copymasters: C43–44

Discussing the text

- Tell children that they are going to read a review of an imaginary novel by an imaginary author – tell them not to try looking for the book in the library!
- Read the review on Resource Book pages 44 and 45.
- *Which sections of the review are fact and which are opinion?*
- *Is this the kind of review which makes you want to read the book? Why?*
- *Can you spot the missing punctuation in the first paragraph?* (There should be a comma after 'Like most of his previous books'.)
- Focus on punctuation generally and in particular the way the quotation is punctuated with speech marks and ellipsis.

Shared Writing

Teacher demonstration

- *I want us to go through the review and see if we can establish its structure or the way it is written.* Write the words 'Introductory paragraph' at the top of your paper.
- *What this paragraph is doing is telling the reader the title of the book, its genre and who wrote it.* Write 'includes title, author, genre' next to or under the paragraph heading (see the Shared Writing Example opposite).
- *They don't have to be written in that order, of course. The reviewer could have written something like: 'Like most of his previous books, P. C. Johns' latest novel is a fantasy with a detection theme entitled "Moonlight and Mothballs".'*

Teacher scribing

- Write 'Paragraph 2'. Ask children what this paragraph is about. *Yes, it's a short summary of what the novel is about.* Write the paragraph label.
- Go through the rest of the review, paragraph by paragraph. Ask children what each paragraph is about and write appropriate labels – see the Shared Writing Example.
- Explain to children that this is the structure they should use in writing about a book or story. Point out the usefulness of using quotations to support statements.

Supported composition

- *Is the review we have read a favourable one? Does the reviewer like the book?*
- *I want us to imagine that the reviewer did not like the book and to write what he or she might have written then. Would we need to change what is written on page 44? No, because that is fact – the details of the book and what it is about are still the same whether a reviewer likes them or not. We have to change all the rest because that is opinion. Remember, that even though this is an unfavourable review there might still be some things the reviewer likes!*
- Remind children what paragraph 3 has to be about by referring to your structure list. Point out that as this is an imaginary novel, they can create additional characters if they like. Ask them to discuss in pairs what the reviewer might have said and then write a brief paragraph.
- Sample the children's writing. Select/amend/amalgamate and scribe.
- Repeat this process for paragraphs 4 and 5. Again, because it is an imaginary novel, children can make up what they want with regard to the novel and the way in which it is written.
- Read the whole review together.

Independent Writing

- Children use Copymaster C4 to review a novel or story they have read recently. Alternatively, they could write about another imaginary novel – which they may find more interesting and which could then be displayed under a heading of 'Books you will never get to read!'

Checking Children's Learning

- Share some of the reviews with the class.
- Is there a clear distinction between the factual part of the review and the opinions?
- Have children used any quotations to support what they are saying?

Revisiting the Objective

- Using the structure headings from Copymaster C4, write a review together of one of the stories/extracts in the Resource Book.

Write a polished poem from a model

Writing objective

T11: To use performance poems as models to write and to produce poetry in polished forms through revising, redrafting and presentation

Text Copymasters: C45–46

Discussing the text

- Before they see the text, tell the children that they are going to read a poem called 'The Sound Collector' (by Roger McGough) and ask them what they think it might be about.
- Read the poem together – you should read the first two verses yourself to establish the rhythm and expression.
- Identify the rhyming scheme (ABCB).
- Ask if the children found that the lack of punctuation helped or hindered them in their reading.
- Ask for suggestions as to how the poem could be read aloud for performance, e.g. individuals or groups reading certain lines or verses.
- Read the poem again in this way.

Shared Writing

Teacher demonstration

- Tell children that you are going to use the idea of someone collecting something to write a poem all together and the poem will be called 'The Word Collector'.
- Write the first verse (Shared Writing Example 1 – opposite). Read it aloud and change 'took' to 'carried', e.g. *I think I'm going to change this to 'carried' because it fits the rhythm better.* Discuss your rhyming scheme (AABB).
- Shared Writing Example 2 is Wendy Body's genuine first draft. She got to the end of the third line, having decided to rhyme 'bun' with 'sun' and then realised she was a total fool and had used the wrong rhyming scheme! You can do the same with the children (hopefully they will spot it before you "realise") or go straight to Shared Writing Example 3.
- Shared Writing Example 3: *We've now got to think about what words the Dictionary Maker is going to collect. I've decided that the next verse will be about him collecting words to do with the spring …*
- Read the two verses together.

Teacher scribing

- Tell the children that the next verse will be about summer. Ask for suggestions for words related to summer and list them separately, e.g. holiday, sand, swimming pool, ice-cream.
- Look for any that rhyme or rhymes you can make, e.g. 'pool' and 'cool', 'summer theme' and 'ice cream', 'play' and 'holiday'.
- Take suggestions for lines, discuss and scribe.
- See if the children (or you) can suggest changes to improve any lines.
- Repeat for the autumn verse.

Shared Writing Example

1. The Word Collector
    The Dictionary Maker came today
    And ~~took~~ carried our favourite words away,
    He cried as he put them in his sack,
    "It's not for long – they will be back!"

2. In went daffodil, ~~next~~ then in went spring,
    ~~Followed by~~ In went Easter, hot, cross and bun
    Followed by primrose and chocolate egg

3. In went daffodil, then in went spring,
    And eggs and Easter, hymns and sing,
    Then he took primrose, hot cross bun,
    Nest and lamb, followed by shine and sun.

4. Life has been dull and speech has been grey,
    Ever since he took those words away;
    Then today we opened our mouths and learned
    That our favourite words have now returned!

Supported composition

- Orally, brainstorm words for the winter verse.
- Ask children to write two rhyming lines on their whiteboards.
- Take examples, select and scribe. If children have written really good lines, do more than one verse, using to begin with: 'Then he took winter and that was worse –/ So many words it takes more than one verse!'

Teacher demonstration

- Add a final verse as in Shared Writing Example 4, then read and perform the poem.

Independent Writing

- Children draft and revise their own poems called 'The Memory Collector'. Base the first verse on the poem you have written together, i.e. 'The Memory Taker came today / And took my favourite memories away, / He cried as he put them in his sack, / "It's not for long – they will be back!"

Checking Children's Learning

- Take examples and discuss how children tackled the task. Compare some first and final drafts. Why did they make the changes?

Revisiting the Objective

- Together, write and revise a poem about 'The Smells Collector' or 'The Sights Collector'.

Term 3 Unit of work 20:

Rewrite a poem in standard English

Writing objective

T11: To produce poetry in polished forms through revising, redrafting and presentation

Links to sentence/word level work

S1: To secure the basic conventions of Standard English

Text Copymaster: C46

Discussing the text

- Tell the children that you are about to read them a poem which is written as if it is a girl talking about her brother.
- Read the poem 'My Bruvver' (page 48).
- *What does 'daffy' mean?*
- *Is it a humorous poem? Why?*
- *Is the poem in standard English like it says at the top of the page?*

Shared Writing

Teacher demonstration

- Clip the acetate sheet over the poem on page 48.
- Tell the children that they are going to be changing the poem and turning it into standard English. So first of all you are going to underline all the things which are not standard English.
- *The first thing to underline is the title 'My Bruvver'. Some people might pronounce 'Brother' like that but it is not the correct spelling is it?*
- *Look at the first line. This is what is called a double negative. What the girl means is that her brother doesn't know anything. But that's not what she says* (because if he doesn't know <u>nothing</u>, then he must know <u>something</u>!) Underline 'don't' and 'nothing'.

Teacher scribing

- Go through the rest of the poem, asking children to identify all the examples of non-standard English for you to underline. Some you may have to point out, e.g. 'off of'. Merely identify and don't correct at this stage.

Independent Writing

- Give out copies of Copymaster C46.
- Children should change the examples of non-standard English into standard English. Keep the underlined text on view in case they need to refer to it.

Teacher scribing

- Ask children for their changes and add these to the underlined text.
- Read through the annotated poem. Identify if and where the changes have interfered with the rhythm and line length.
- Take suggestions as to how the standard English version of the poem might be improved. (See the 'translation' in the Shared Writing Example.) Suggestions should also include punctuation.
- Amend the poem accordingly.

Shared Writing Example

My <u>Bruvver</u>	My **Brother**
He <u>don't</u> know <u>nothing</u> <u>not</u> nothing at all, Only a fool like <u>what</u> he is could fall <u>off of</u> that wall!	He doesn't know anything, He knows nothing at all: Only a fool like my brother Could fall off that wall!
He <u>ain't</u> got <u>no</u> sense His <u>brains gotta</u> be slim <u>I never seen nobody</u> Who's as <u>daffy</u> as him.	He just has no sense, His brain has to be slim – I've never seen anyone As stupid as him.
We <u>was</u> going to <u>pinch</u> apples <u>What was</u> close to that wall Till my <u>bruvver</u> fell <u>off of</u> – Now <u>we got none</u> at all!	We were after the apples Which were close to the wall Till my brother fell off Now we've got none at all!

Independent Writing

- Children should work as a group to write a conversation poem (it doesn't have to rhyme) between the girl and her brother where she is accusing and he is defending and retaliating. They should see how much non-standard English they can get into the poem. *This is your chance to write in very bad English for once!*
- Once the new non-standard English poems have been written, swap them among the groups.
- Each group should then write a standard English version of the poem they have been given.
- Display the poems in standard and non-standard English pairs.

Checking Children's Learning

- Go through the poems checking that children are able to articulate *why* various changes have had to be made.

Revisiting the Objective

- Draw up a standard English chart with the class for display, e.g:

Non-standard English	Standard English
• He <u>don't</u> know <u>nothing</u>	• He doesn't know anything • He knows nothing
• like <u>what</u> he is	• like he is
•	•

Paragraph	Content	The Author's Purpose

Cast or Cast List
- the list of actors or characters
- placed at the beginning of the play
- often includes explanatory notes about characters

Acts
- the main sections into which plays are divided
- numbered sequentially

Scenes
- the numbered sections or divisions within an act
- a new scene starts when there is a change of time or place – usually a brief note about the setting after the heading e.g. Scene 1: The castle, later that night

Speeches
- need to sound like people talking
- often use contracted verb forms e.g. "isn't", "I'm"

Narrator
- a member of the cast but does not take part in the action
- acts as a storyteller to explain, comment or give information which would be difficult or take too long to get across in characters' speeches

Stage Directions
- explanations or instructions within the playscript to actors about movements or how to speak
- usually written as notes and not complete sentences – usually printed in italics with brackets

Production Notes
- information and suggestions about how to stage or perform the play
- can be hand-written annotations on a playscript or printed separately at the end

Layout
- speakers' names are in bold type or capital letters
- placed on the left-hand side of the page as if in a margin
- space between speaker's name and his/her speech
- speeches are never written with speech marks
- one line's space between speeches

Myths, legends and folktales are different kinds of ancient story.
Their key features are described in the chart below.

Myths	Legends	Folktales
usually stories which have been handed down over the years in a particular culture or mix of cultures	usually stories which have been handed down over the years in a particular culture or mix of cultures	usually stories which have been handed down over the years in a particular culture or mix of cultures
frequently give glimpses of their country of origin, e.g. in their physical settings, traditions, clothes	frequently give glimpses of their country of origin, e.g. in their physical settings, traditions, clothes	frequently give glimpses of their country of origin, e.g. in their physical settings, traditions, clothes
often existed and changed by word of mouth before they were written down	usually existed and changed by word of mouth before they were written down	usually existed and changed by word of mouth before they were written down
came about as people used their imaginations to create stories to explain: – the existence of human beings – human behaviour and beliefs – the forces of nature – different aspects of the natural world	stories which generally feature human heroes and heroines and present ideals of virtue and bravery (often involves fighting beasts, monsters or non-humans)	generally about good triumphing over evil in some shape or form and virtue always being rewarded
generally feature supernatural beings: gods. goddesses who help or control the human or animal characters	the heroes and plots may be based on real people or events but they have been greatly exaggerated and added to over the years	often contain these elements: – youngest son as hero – use of three (e.g. 3 days 3 wishes, 3 brothers) – someone who hides their true identity

Introductory paragraph   *include title, author, genre*

Paragraph 2   *short summary of the story*

Paragraph 3   *how the characters are portrayed*

Paragraph 4   *features of the author's style (use quotes?)*

Paragraph 5   *own views and reactions; what others might think*

Viola Angotti

It had been one of those suggestions that stuns everyone with its rightness. Someone had said, "Hey, let's put those girls over there in the trash cans!" and the plan won immediate acceptance. Nothing could have been more appropriate. The trash cans were big and had just been emptied, and in an instant the boys were off chasing the girls and yelling at the tops of their lungs.

It had been wonderful at first, Mouse remembered. Primitive blood had raced through his body. The desire to capture had driven him like a wild man through the school yard, up the sidewalk, everywhere. He understood what had driven the cave man and the barbarian, because this same passion was driving him. Putting the girls in the trash cans was the most important challenge of his life. His long screaming charge ended with him red-faced, gasping for breath – and Viola Angotti pinned against the garbage cans.

He called again, "Come on, you guys, get the lid off this garbage can, will you?"

And then, when he said that, Viola Angotti had taken two steps forward. She said, "Nobody's putting me in no garbage can." He could still remember how she had looked standing there. She had recently taken the part of the Statue of Liberty in a class play, and somehow she seemed taller and stronger at this moment than when she had been in costume.

He cried, "Hey, you guys!" It was a plea. "Where are you?"

And then Viola Angotti had taken one more step, and with a faint sigh she had socked him in the stomach so hard that he had doubled over and lost his lunch. He hadn't known it was possible to be hit like that outside a boxing ring. It was the hardest blow he had ever taken. Viola Angotti could be heavyweight champion of the world.

As she walked past his crumpled body she said again, "Nobody's putting me in no garbage can." It had sounded like one of the world's basic truths. The sun will rise. The tides will flow. Nobody's putting Viola Angotti in the garbage can.

Extract from *The Eighteenth Emergency* by Betsy Byars

Units of work 1, 2 and 13

Writing a Reading Journal

Describe

What story genre is this?
What is this chapter about?
Where is the story taking place?
Who is telling the story?
What are these characters like?
Is there anything special about the way the author uses language?

Predict

What do I think will happen next?
Can I guess who is going to be the villain?
Can I guess how the character will handle this problem?
Is this character going to change? How?
How will the story end?
How far was my prediction correct?

Question

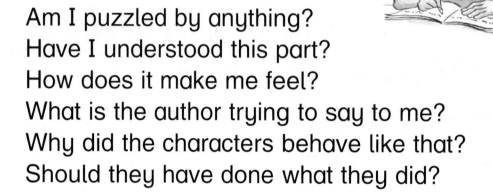

Am I puzzled by anything?
Have I understood this part?
How does it make me feel?
What is the author trying to say to me?
Why did the characters behave like that?
Should they have done what they did?

Reflect

How would I have handled this problem
or situation?
Does this remind me of anything?
Is the mood of the story changing?
What do I like about the author's style?
What did I think about the ending?

Evacuee

The slum had been his home since he
　　was born;
And then the war came, and he was
　　rudely torn
From all he'd ever known; and with his
　　case
Of mean necessities, brought to a place
Of silences and space; just boom of sea
And sough of wind; small wonder then
　　that he

Unit of work 4

Crept out one night to seek his sordid slum,

And thought to find his way. By dawn
   he'd come

A few short miles; and cattle in their herds

Gazed limpidly as he trudged by, and birds

Just stirring in first light, awoke to hear

His lonely sobbing, born of abject fear

Of sea and hills and sky; of silent night

Unbroken by the sound of shout and fight.

Edith Pickthall

Writing Metaphors

The hungry tide
gobbled up the beach.

The branches swayed
dreamily in a slow
stately dance.

He had eyes of flint
and a heart of stone.

The baby's skin was
peaches and cream.

Hailstones hurled
themselves in anger
against the window pane.

The cottage snuggled
comfortably in the
arms of the hills.

Unit of work 5

Making up Metaphors ...

The wind   **A building**

A tree   **An evil person**

Pelican Shared Writing Year 5 Fiction © Pearson Education Limited 2001

Act 3: Inside the Labyrinth

Periboea (as narrator)

That night, Ariadne went to see Theseus ...

Ariadne **Theseus, I want to help you kill that dreadful monster. Look what I've brought.**

Theseus **A ball of string? What use is that?**

Ariadne **It is enchanted string. Tie it to the doorpost of the Labyrinth.**

It will unwind itself,
and lead you to the
Minotaur. When you
have killed it, follow
the string back to
the entrance!

Theseus Why are you helping
me? Your father would
kill you if he knew.

Units of work 6, 7 and 8

Ariadne **When I saw you coming off the ship, I fell in love with you. I will help you, but you must promise to take me back to Athens and marry me!**

Periboea (as narrator)

Theseus agreed. Soon after, the guards came to take him to the Labyrinth.

Hermus (as narrator)

Once inside the vast maze, no one had ever found their way out again.

Units of work 6, 7 and 8

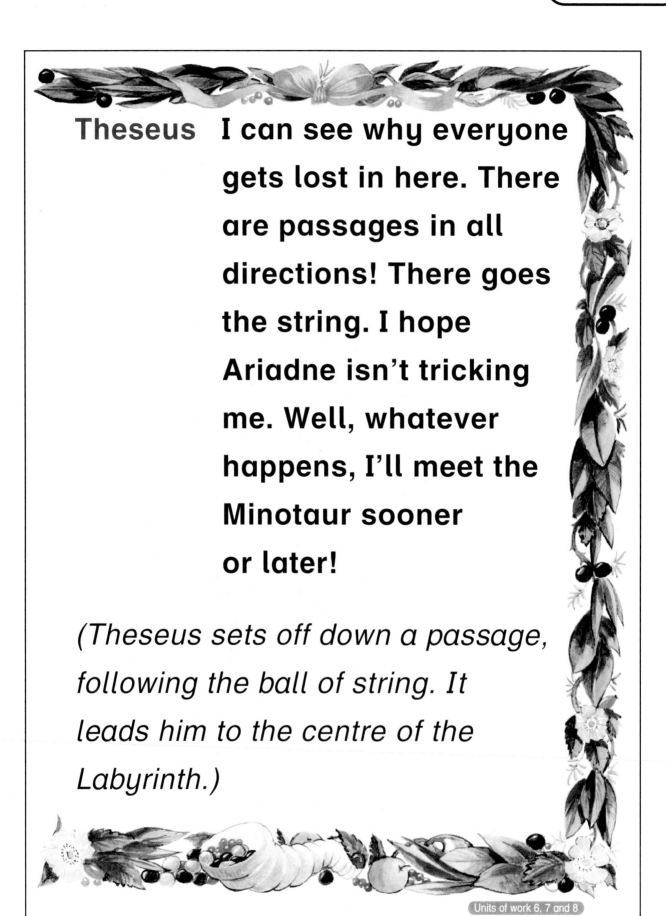

Theseus I can see why everyone gets lost in here. There are passages in all directions! There goes the string. I hope Ariadne isn't tricking me. Well, whatever happens, I'll meet the Minotaur sooner or later!

(Theseus sets off down a passage, following the ball of string. It leads him to the centre of the Labyrinth.)

Units of work 6, 7 and 8

Asterion *(under his breath)* **Here comes my next victim!** *(To Theseus)* **Get ready to die!**

Units of work 6, 7 and 8

What will happen next?

What stages will the fight go through?

- **Theseus responds to what Asterion has said**

-

How the fight between Theseus and Asterion will be portrayed:
- dialogue (D)
- stage directions (SD)
- described by the narrators (N)

Annotate the stages above.

Tee-rah-wah's Gift

Long, long ago, when the buffalo roamed the grasslands of America, Kenu lived alone with his mother for his father had been killed while hunting. One night, his mother became ill; Kenu, running to fetch help, fell and broke his leg.

With the help of Medicine Man and members of the tribe, Kenu's leg slowly improved ... but, sadly, his mother died.

Units of work 9, 10 and 11

Pelican Shared Writing Year 5 Fiction © Pearson Education Limited 2001

When Spring came, Kenu was unable to set out on the long trek to hunt buffalo with the rest of the tribe; he sat by the river and watched as they left the village. Alone and dispirited, he picked up a handful of wet clay and idly began to shape it.

Units of work 9, 10 and 11

He decided to model a dog but somehow the legs were too long – as was the head and the tail. He tried again but the second model was just like the first. It was as if someone was guiding his hands. Kenu took the two strange animals home and placed them in his hut. That night he dreamed ...

In his dream, the great god Tee-rah-wah appeared saying, "It was I who guided you to make these animals which I have named horses. Take them to the river so that they may eat and drink. Do this for four days and then they will be fully grown."

Kenu woke and looked at the little animals. They were alive and scampering around the hut! He did as Tee-rah-wah had commanded and by the end of the first day the horses were as big as dogs.

By the third day the horses were bigger than Kenu. He got on the back of one of them and, clinging to its mane, he rode it along the bank of the river. "With you I am as fast as the wind!" Kenu cried excitedly. His weak leg would no longer prevent him from going hunting.

Units of work 9, 10 and 11

On the fourth day, he couldn't wait to show the horses to the rest of the tribe and set off to find them. He forgot that the horses should have been taken to the river once more.

Tee-rah-wah was disappointed: he had wanted to give the tribe big, powerful horses. But then he saw how fast they ran, how easily and quickly they turned. Realising that the small, fast horses would be ideal for hunting buffalo, Tee-rah-wah smiled and was content.

Wendy Body

Units of work 9, 10 and 11

Overheard on a saltmarsh

Nymph, nymph, what are your beads?

Green glass, goblin. Why do you stare at them?

Give them me.

No.

Give them me. Give them me.

No.

Then I will howl all night in the reeds,
Lie in the mud and howl for them.

Goblin, why do you love them so?

They are better than stars or water,
Better than voices of winds that sing,
Better than any man's fair daughter,
Your green glass beads on a silver ring.

Hush, I stole them out of the moon.

Give me your beads, I want them.

No.

I will howl in a deep lagoon

For your green glass beads, I love
them so.

Give them me. Give them me.

No.

Harold Monro

What Do All Stories Have?

Physical, temporal, cultural settings:

Where and when does it all happen?
Is there a particular country or culture?

Main and secondary characters

What role does each character have?
Who are the important ones?

First or third person narrative

Who is telling the story?

An opening or introduction

How is the reader's attention caught?

Initiating event:

What starts everything off? Is there a
problem? Does something go wrong?

Response/reaction

What happens because of this?

Action–reaction pattern is repeated:

What happens as a result of that?

Climax

What is the high point of the action?

Resolution

How is the problem solved? What makes everything turn out right in the end?

Message or moral

Does the main character learn anything or change in any way? Can the reader learn something from the story?

Pelican Shared Writing Year 5 Fiction © Pearson Education Limited 2001

Revising Writing

Revising comes from "re-vision" which means seeing again ...

 You can CHECK that standard story features have been included.

 You can ADD words to make the meaning clearer or create detail.

 You can CHANGE words to be more exact or to have more effect.

 'You can DELETE unnecessary words to tighten up sentences.

 You can REARRANGE words, sentences or paragraphs to make things link better, improve the flow or to have more impact.

Unit of work 13

You can ALTER sentence structures to make the style more interesting and varied.

 You can INVENT similes and metaphors to improve descriptions.

 You can IMPROVE punctuation to help the reader with the meaning.

 You can CORRECT obvious mistakes or slips of the pen.

Pelican Shared Writing Year 5 Fiction © Pearson Education Limited 2001

Counting the Stars

It's late at night

and John is counting the stars

he's walking through the woods

and counting the stars.

The night is clear

and the stars are like salt

on a black table cloth.

John counts silently,

his lips moving, his head tilted.

It's late at night

and John is counting the stars

until he walks into a tree

that he never saw

because he was counting the stars.

Look at John
lying in the woods.

The woodland creatures are gathering
around him laughing.

in little woodland voices.

MORAL: Even when you're looking up,
Don't forget to look down.

Ian McMillan

Unit of work 14

Something wrong with the stove?

Pongo and Missis both knew that humans did not like dogs to go into buildings which had towers and tall, narrow windows. They had no idea why, and had at first been a little hurt when told firmly to wait outside. But Mrs Dearly had once said: "We would love you to come in if it were allowed. And I would go in far oftener if you could." So it was obviously one of those mysterious things such as no one – not even humans – ever being allowed to walk on certain parts of the grass in Regent's Park.

"We must get them out quickly," said Pongo, "and go on with our journey."

Units of work 15, 16 and 17

Units of work 15, 16 and 17

They soon found the door in the tower – which the biggest pups had pushed wide open. Because Missis had always been left outside, she disliked these curious buildings with towers and high windows; but the minute she got inside, she changed her mind. This was a wonderful place – so peaceful and, somehow, so welcoming.

309
427
221
135
108

"But where are the pups?" she said, peering all around.

She saw lots of black patches on the moonlit floor but had quite forgotten that all the pups were now black. Then she remembered and as she drew nearer to the sleeping pups, tears sprang to her eyes.

Units of work 15, 16 and 17

"Look, look at all the puppy beds!" she cried. "What good people must live here!"

"It can't be the kind of place I thought it was," said Pongo.

He was about to wake the puppies when Missis stopped him.

"Let me sit by the stove for a little while," she said.

"Not too long, my dear," said Pongo.

He need not have worried. Missis only sat still for a few minutes. Then she got up, shook herself, and said brightly;

"Let us start now. Things are going to be all right."

An hour or so later, just before the evening service, the Verger said to the Vicar:

"I think there must be something wrong with the stove, sir."

On every hassock he had found a small, circular patch of soot.

From *One Hundred and One Dalmatians* by Dodie Smith

Units of work 15, 16 and 17

Writing About A Story

"Moonlight and Mothballs" is the latest novel by P. C. Johns. Like most of his previous books it is a fantasy with a detection theme.

Moonlight discovers that wearing her granny's old fur coat (which smells of mothballs) gives her great powers. With it, she is able to travel back into the past and solve the mystery of the missing Crown Jewels.

Unit of work 18

The rather zany Moonlight is an appealing main character – especially when she tackles the villain, Sideways Sid, when she finally tracks him down. Sideways Sid, with his amazing ability to slip through small spaces, is an equally strong and life-like character.

P. C. Johns is a writer with an eye for detail who makes good use of imagery to bring characters and settings to life: "... Sideways Sid, skulking with all the grace of a three-legged cat ..."

Some readers may find that the novel takes a little while to get going but others will appreciate the slow build-up to the moment when the Crown Jewels are found to be missing. From there, things move at a great pace!

The Sound Collector

A stranger called this morning
Dressed all in black and grey
put every sound into a bag
And carried them away

The whistling of the kettle
The turning of the lock
The purring of the kitten
The ticking of the clock

The popping of the toaster
The crunching of the flakes
When you spread the marmalade
The scraping noise it makes

The hissing of the frying-pan
The ticking of the grill
The bubbling of the bathtub
As it starts to fill

Unit of work 19

The drumming of the raindrops
On the window-pane
When you do the washing-up
The gurgle of the drain

The crying of the baby
The squeaking of the chair
The swishing of the curtain
The creaking of the stair

A stranger called this morning
He didn't leave his name
Left us only silence
Life will never be the same.

Roger McGough

Unit of work 19

Standard English

My Bruvver

He don't know nothing
not nothing at all,
Only a fool like what he is
could fall off of that wall!

He ain't got no sense
His brains gotta be slim
I never seen nobody
Who's as daffy as him.

We was going to pinch apples
What was close to that wall
Till my bruvver fell off of –
Now we got none at all!

Wendy Body